THE SUNFLOWERS THAT DON'T FOLLOW THE SUN

BIRU PANDA

I created this piece of work to give all my experiences a home. Perhaps, some of you can relate and even have similar insights. I love to pen down, not just because it's a form of expression, but also because it's another language to me that I love.

To my readers, thank you for your support over the years. This book is dedicated to you all for reading my work. The best moments I have with you is when you interpret my work from a different perspective and I have come to love that process of creating something that gives different meanings to different people. Because that's how art should be, subjective.

Contents

Contents

Acknowledgements

To my supportive friends and family, I wouldn't have done this without you.

To my friend Aditya Biswas, thank you for editing my write-ups. You always have my back.

To my friends who helped me select the write-ups, i'm glad to have you all around to publish this piece of work.

1. The Sky Knows Where We Met

The very first time I realised
we live under the same sky
was when I saw all the stars in your eyes.

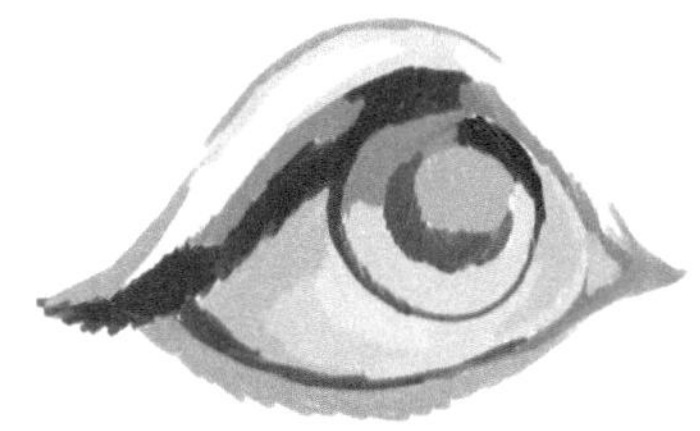

You're the chapter in my book I couldn't end.
And so, the story goes on.
You see, there is no possible scenario in my head
where you just disappear.

And so,

I write it all down on a piece of paper

wanting to forget you

and set it on fire.

But why do I feel my heart burning instead?

• 4 •

We die several times, don't we?
Everytime we see the world in a new way,
our old self dies a little.
The only way it can revive is when
we meet someone from our past.
And when we forget about them,
we no longer breathe the same fire of our past.

"So, what if I can't forget certain people?"
"You grow apart until one of you does."

2. The Secrets Of My Universe

I know you don't dream of me.
When I asked the stars
to send you a letter,
they replied they can only
carry a message for the people
who dream about each other in their sleep.

You still have a key to my door.
I wonder if I'll find you home someday
and have to call you a stranger again.

Oh, how the sky watched you pen about hope
when you didn't have an ounce of it.

Doesn't it get tiring to be the star that never twinkles?
To be the guide that leads people in the dark?
I've heard of stories where you don't sleep
unless the sun arrives on the horizon.
Even then you still shine for a few people
who need you in the daylight.

It is a mystery
how I can see so much of myself
when I look into your eyes
than when I look in a mirror.

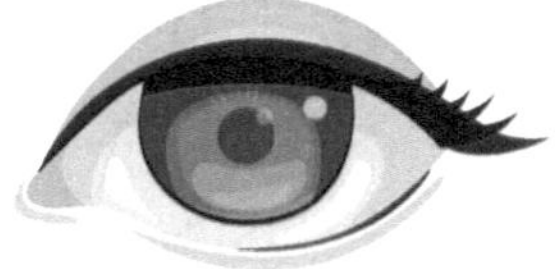

—

"I renamed the stars when you didn't return home."

- Biru Panda

3. The Missing Clouds

I regret telling the
clouds about you.
The sky makes a familiar face
when it smiles.

• 14 •

We're clouds from different winds,
destined to meet one day.
But we've to keep colliding into others
until I reach you.

If every cloud was a different person,
they would be my summary of everything.
The pictures of clouds in my gallery
have a lot of stories to tell.

The sun
has been hiding
behind the clouds
ever since I had a taste for light.

But how can you
hide the stars from not shining?
Even in the darkest of nights
where the sky appears
to be a blank patch,
the stars in the far end
find a spot in the canvas.

4. November Yearnings

There is no way
destiny is so small
that it can not contain
all the people's dreams.

Destiny awaits for people
who can stop history
from repeating itself.

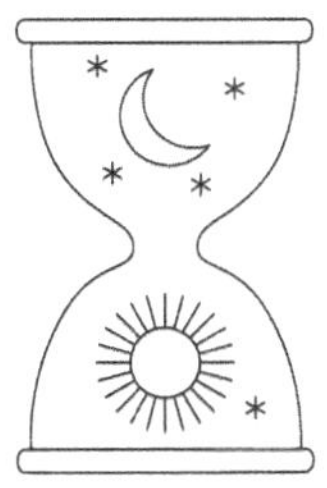

I hope you take a leap.
I hope you're not afraid
of the height you climb everyday.
I hope you're not guilty when you look back.
After all, if you don't take the leap,
how will you know how high you can fly?

I don't think fate has a plan for you to rest.
It wants you back on your feet
before the world starts to move faster around you.
The light might seem too bright now
but it's better to move towards it
than wait in misery for it to diminish.

The leaves don't wish to turn yellow.
Yet, they fall when autumn drives past.
When it's time,
we all leave our branches, don't we?
We all have places to be before the season changes.

No, destiny does not wait for you.
Waiting for destiny to offer you a chance
is like waiting in the railway station.
Half the time you don't know when it's going to arrive,
your destination might change mid-way
and maybe a wrong train might
take you to the right destination.

—

"I was raised between the seasons, winter and summer. For a brief amount of time I was named spring but that wasn't fair to the chaos I brought."

- Biru Panda

5. The Blue Candle

You are fire
and the only reason
one puts off fire
is because they know
what it can annihilate.

It is said that
when someone's fire isn't kindled
to offer warmth to others,
it tends to leave them burning.

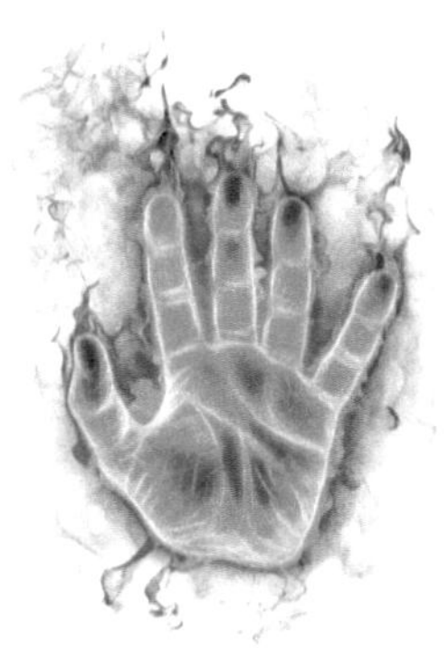

Flame, fire and the smoke-
It starts with something you posses,
to what you do with it
and finally to something
you have to live with.

• 30 •

I light up candles all the way
for you to reach home.
I don't know why you fancy flames so much.
You always were a fire child;
burning the paper
to watch it become a mess,
setting five match sticks on fire at the same time;
your hand is always the closest to the flame
than anyone I know.
Yet, the times I come close to worry about it,
you reach home
and I remember how beautiful
the candle flames look in your eyes.

6. The Eye Of The Storm

If we talked about
strangers in our lives,
would they be the ones
you never talked to
or the ones you used to talk to?

To other people,
it may look like nothing,
but there are pictures in my gallery
that summon me
to early summers of 2012.
I wish I could have warned myself
to not get my heart broken so young from people.

And when something breaks you,
do you get up to face the sun
or enjoy the rainbow?

I try too hard
to make things happen.
And before I know it,
I'm trying too hard
to get rid of it.

Your eyes are beautifully catastrophic.
They've seen so many high tides
and barely dodged them,
escaped disasters in hideouts
and climbed out in the pleasant weather.
But they tell a different story now.
Tell me,
how does it feel to be the eye of the storm?

—

"Maybe the reason you have not found the meaning of life is because there isn't one but multiple ones, its the other way around, maybe what shapes your soul carries the meanings of life, but ofcourse they'll not reveal themselves until the very end. Maybe that's why only few people come very close to learn it, and before they could get a chance to recite it, they vanish away.
And if heaven has a different pass-key for every soul, maybe the meanings you learn would open the gates to eternity."

- Biru Panda

7. The Language of my Muse

I don't get it.
I thought the more I pen about you,
the more I would eventually
run out of things to write.
But somehow while doing this,
I started speaking your language
and I humanly could not find any cure
from making you my muse.

It's hard to unlearn a language
you once spoke;
the language of one's eyes.

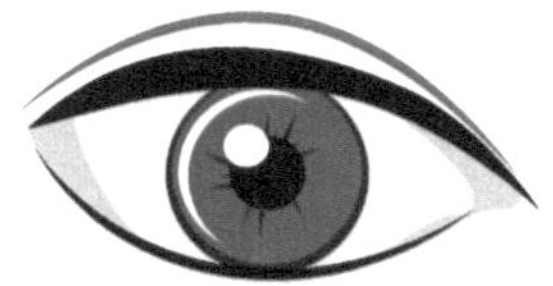

I don't know what to do
with the letters I never posted.
Sometimes they stare at me
for having a part of myself
inside the envelopes.
Should I let them out
or burn them?
It's been so long that
I forget what it's like to have my pieces back.

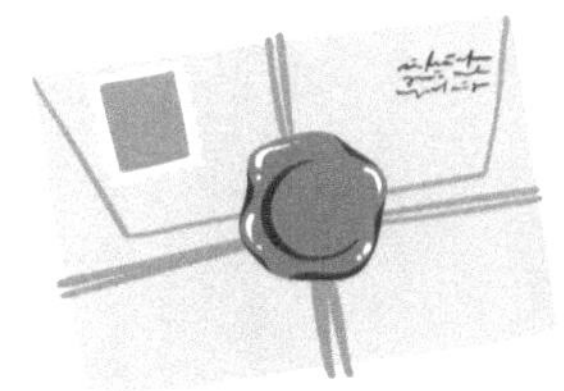

I had left a bookmark
on one of my books you borrowed.
The page was about a character
who subtly hinted at a love spark.
I hoped you would notice it
while flipping through the pages.
Days later, when I got the book back,
it was bookmarked where the character was walking with
someone
with one umbrella.

• 43 •

If I had known
you turned the flowers I got you
into flattened ones inside your favourite books,
I would have planted a whole garden for you.

8. The Concept Of A Human

Humans are concepts.
We're not always defined as people
but by what values we bring to the table.
We're entities who keep defining ourselves innumerable times.
And so, if someone defines us by our old values,
that won't be valid anymore.

We're able to forget someone
who was close to us
because we unlearn their concepts.
We're not forgetting them as a person.
We would still recognise them if we run into that person,
but we don't define them by the same concept as we used to.

You can't love a person;
it would last forever effortlessly.
I don't think we ever fall a person,
but for an idea of them.
That's why they turn out to be different
from who we thought they are.

It's no wonder people can't define you.
You're a concept.
You're not meant to be defined so easily.
People think you're often lost,
but I think you're only exploring.

• 48 •

Concepts are immortal
and so are you;
in the million ways you inspire someone,
motivate them,
show them light,
hear their tragedies,
help out souls,
close other's wounds,
fight for them,
you get to live on as a concept in their darkest times.

—

"If heaven looks different for everyone, in whose heaven shall I find myself?"

- Biru Panda

9. The Language Of Poetry

Poetry is a secret language.
It can carry numerous meanings and perspectives
and perhaps only a few can know
what it intends to say.
But isn't that the whole point,
to speak a language
not known to every single soul?

I write a poem for you,

and to be able to be true to every word I pen down,

I leave a part of me inside the letter.

I let you borrow it;

I feel a void inside me.

I wait for your letter to replenish my other half.

And weeks later, I receive a reply.

I like your letters; they're neat.

You probably never once forgot to put the stamp, unlike me.

But the only thing you forgot to attach to this letter

was a part of you.

•53•

Sometimes, I think of burning my old letters.

They're overly descriptive of my feelings.

When I was small,

I simply wrote what I felt in the most kiddish manner.

Interesting, how I grew up learning new words

to mask my emotions.

Not many can know what I truly mean to say,

not many can realise where the paragraph is leading to.

On some occasions,

I write just to understand myself.

At first, when I was trying poetry,
I wasn't thinking from my heart.
I was trying so hard to make it rhyme
that one day I completely ran out of them.
But poetry is a secret language, isn't it?
It never occurred to me,
poetry is a language of grief,
the world of What If's and 'almost' to someone,
the words that never escaped from my mouth
but from my pen.
And then, I knew poetry.

People are told to write a letter
for their future selves;
you may come across people
who give up on you
but you shouldn't be the one
who stops believing in yourself.

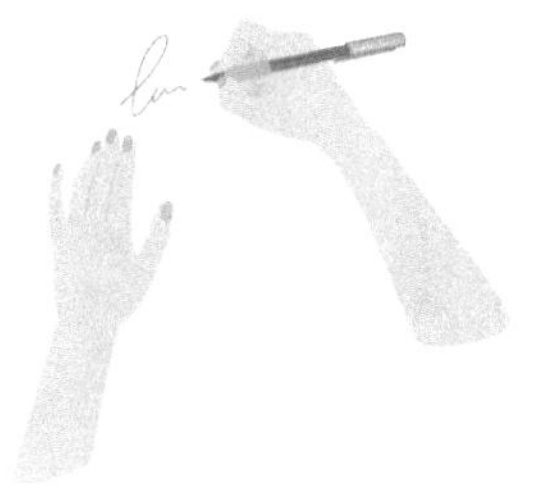

10. Dreams Of My Sonnets

I only remember dreams in my sleep.
I wake up with no details in reality.
But the next day when I had a dream,
I seemed to remember the context again.
I only remember dreams in my sleep.

I need a continuation of my favourite dreams.
It ends too quickly,
and sometimes wakes me up with a dry throat.
I need to know how it ends,
at least in my dreams.

Why don't we often
dream of things
we love?

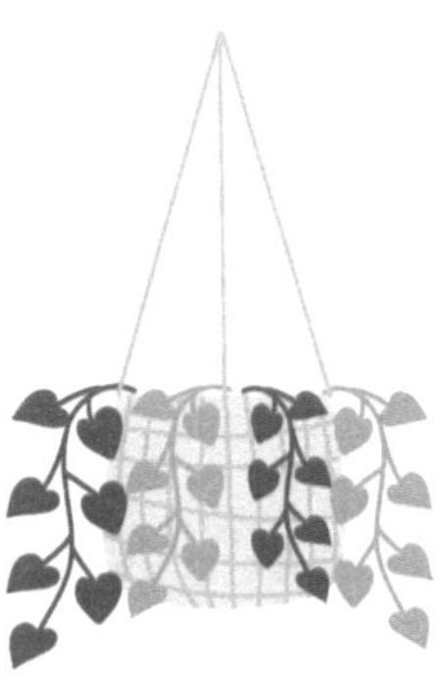

What if all of this is really just a dream,
and that is the reason why
nothing seems to be in your control?

You're waiting to be greeted
by the things that don't let you sleep;
either the nightmares
or your wildest dreams.

—

"It's not the end of the world.
It's the beginning of mine."

- Biru Panda

11. Keepers Of The Heart

I think sometimes,

I want you to magically know

what I want to say;

just look in my eyes

and read my soul.

Perhaps saying it will shatter the daydreams I've been having.

I look at your zodiac when I look at mine.

I want to know when our fates will intertwine.

There's always a faint fear
to tell you what's in my heart.
Every so often,
I highlight a few lines from the book I borrow
or maybe make you a playlist.
I wonder if you look at me because you know now.
I never had the courage
to highlight the part about my aching heart.
I could only highlight the parts you like.

I am afraid to lend you a hug.
I fear that I can't keep my heart quiet
when it's speaking.

I think the language of the heart
is closeness.
It doesn't speak until it finds out
you're not going to be here for long.

I can't seem to distinguish you from my dreams.

I always want to be with you,

so much so that,

it transcends the reality of not being able to be with you.

You ask me if dreams ever come true;

but why does one reality has to be the same as the other?

12. Comfort Is Not My Home

We all grow
in the absence of comfort.
We all heal
in the presence of comfort.

Comfort is the shop around the street
that you go on weekends.
She only knows you by the days you visit.
But she doesn't know your name.
You've never spent quite a time there to be acquainted.
Everytime you make the Shopkeeper's Bell ring,
she knows you're not here for long.

—

"What more interesting can people offer if not the chapters from their lives."

- Biru Panda

13. Harbinger Of Change

I am used to keeping old things.
I can not discard memories.
It starts with making space in my room to place them
and ends with taking up a tiny room inside me.
And when I walk in there,
it is like stepping into a forest-
confusing, old and scary.

Sometimes, I wish to burn the forest of memories
and give rise to new ones from the ashes.
Yet the times I get a false alarm about a fire,
every fibre in my body tries to put off the fire before it
happens.

The forest is only visible at night.
Before I walk in,
I see the harbinger of change before me.
He warns me,
this is not the right way
but I keep walking inside.
Sometimes, I forget what I'm looking for in the forest
and pick up something I obsess over for days.

The harbinger tells me

that sunlight exists in the real world

where moments haven't turned into memories yet.

Once the moment has passed,

few of them make it to the forest.

It is haunting that one can not exist without the other's

presence.

• 77 •

I think we keep visiting the forest
to look back on our past selves.
Sometimes we visit to re-live memories,
and other times to get wounded again,
because we seem to forget
the sunlight doesn't reach there anymore.

14. Where The World Begins

You don't have to be at your absolute worst
to start loving yourself.
Instead, love yourself in every step,
and not just because there's no one else around to do that
but because it's a privilege to be taken care of
by the same hands which once ruined you.

"If there was a way to go back
and start everything differently,
would you do it?",
I asked myself looking at the mirror.
My reflection hasn't been same since then.

I am home
to both the darkness and the light.
Sadly, I can only carry either in my eyes.

• 81 •

"Why is it so cold inside your heart?"
"Because it often rains in here."
"Do you love the rain?"
"I wait for the rainbows."

15. Looking For Chaos

On silent evenings,
I feel an emptiness
big enough to fit everything I've ever felt.
And by the time the sun sets,
I would regret giving them a home.

The meaning of life
is hidden in the broken things.
You can replace old memories
yet you can't change the lesson in it.

I am home to all the things

I've ever loved,

even the things I don't want now.

Yet, I hold them close

thinking if I need them soon and so,

I end up complaining about the space in my heart forever.

You've made a home
from the matchsticks you never burned,
waiting for someone to set it on fire.
You were never looking for warmth.
You were waiting to get a reason
to step out of your own cage.

—

"Imagination will take you to many fascinating places, more often to somewhere you don't think you belong - to your old house with memories or maybe to your lover's arms.

And among them, there lies a feeling that you can't call a home anymore."

- Biru Panda

16. Close To Your Eyes

I love your eyes
and how it sees the world.
The same doomed world I hate living in,
seems bearable in your eyes.
They have fear and disappointment
but also dreamlands and compassion.
Yet those eyes never long to be understood
since the day you discovered no one sees the world like you
did.
Your eyes are so beautiful
that I could almost fall for myself.

You have an ocean of grief in your eyes.
The waves ride so high,
the sand castles on the shore gets washed away easily.
Everytime you push yourself away from the shore,
the waves inch in on you along with a shade only I recognise;
your eyes take the color of the grief you carry.

Eyes have their own language,
the entirety of human emotion
is portrayed by the eyes first,
and sometimes it can't be contained within mere words.

I think light reflects a little differently on your eyes.

Even on the most gloomiest of days,

when I hold your hands,

your eyes still shine the same.

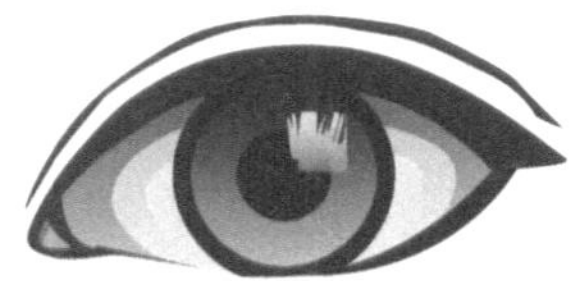

Eyes are the doorway to one's soul.
If you know what the eyes say,
you know they can't lie.

17. Memories That Never Fade

When I asked you to stay,
you had no intention of staying.
But I think my heart felt empty
long before that.

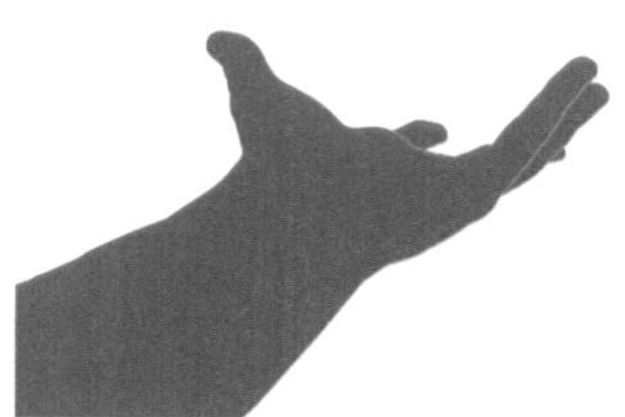

You had become an obsession.
Waking up to your texts,
ending my day with your voice,
getting to know new things about you everyday
and taking just a few extra minutes of your time on our call
was a part of my life.
But, what do you call a person who has become an obsession?
A new home where you can be yourself
or a place where you would hate being alone?

They say sad people write about the past
because they are not over it.
I say they write about the past
because they know they are not alone on this.

People are weirdly complicated.

They dare to leave without letting us know that they are gone.

They vanish from our lives

as mysteriously as they appeared.

And I am left here thinking

what will I do knowing the small things about them.

Perhaps more than people leaving us,
it's the memories that haunt us.
Memories stay when people don't.
And a memory without a person
is essentially a dream without people.
A peaceful dream can haunt you when it's too silent.

18. Naming my Constellation

I find myself stopping between the lines
when I see your name.
The moment I blink,
I know the illusion in my mind will end
and I won't find you between those lines anymore.
I pause to think
if it's really your name I stumbled upon in the book.
But then I whisper to myself,
"If it was really you, I wouldn't be afraid to blink."

I see a glimpse of you in other people.

I'm not sure why it happens,

or why I can't stop it.

Maybe I try to fit the missing puzzle piece

with the people around me,

but it keeps falling out.

And everytime I pick it up again,

the puzzle keeps changing its shape.

Someone's puzzle piece isn't meant to fit another one.

You might think it fits at the right place

but you don't get the right picture.

In fact, it's not even from the same puzzle.

The truth is, we have thousands of puzzle pieces inside us.

With time, we slowly learn which one fits where to make our

identity clear.

And more often than not if a piece doesn't fit anymore,

it's a sign that you're trying too hard to complete the same

picture again.

• 102 •

But we don't always get the same picture as before.

That's why you get newer puzzle pieces.

And if you keep trying to fit the old one in the new picture,

and then again in the newer one,

the picture will get farther and farther away from completing

itself.

No matter how hard you worked on the rest,

one wrong piece can't complete the puzzle.

I think most people get signs about their puzzles.
We can't find all the pieces by ourselves.
And often we follow a sign.
That sign could be missing someone,
and so you follow the piece to add it.
And sometimes it's a sign to replace it
since it doesn't fit no matter how hard you try.

I look for signs in the puzzle
like they look for constellations in stars.
I am searching for something that'll guide me.
Signs are a sign that
you're lost in the first place,
for only the wanderers will be able to see them.

—

"How are we all created from the same stardust and yet rule out the possibility that people need each other for a world with more smiles?"

- Biru Panda

19. We Owe it to the Stars

We met in the summer of 2018. March, as Holi approached, me and my squad coloured each other with the weirdest color combinations possible.

We had walked three kilometres since we started and reached several blocks away from the starting point of celebration. I guess that's what Holi is all about, coloring strangers, dancin' to the street music, visiting friends' places and making their faces unrecognizable.

The friend we visited had invited us over to the apartment who celebrated Holi with grand celebration, music and drinks, Sharbats mostly. The ground floor had a battle of color filled pichkaris and intensely loud music. I don't play Holi that hard, I waited for the things to calm down, so that I would get another one of those Sharbats again.

Separated from friends, I took a seat on the far away lined series of chairs where the audience rested after a long day of Holi. It was crowded. I looked to my right, someone was laughing quietly. I didn't know her, did she know me? I couldn't tell, when everyone was wearing a coloured mask on Holi.

"What?", I asked her with a light smile.

"It's nothing", she continued laughing.

"Tell me", my smile widened, like the times when the laugh is funnier than the joke. I still had no idea what she was smiling about.

"You look like Freud's Model of Psyche."

"Pshych... Psychology stuff?"

"Yes, I'm a psychology student and the way your face is colored reminds me of the Freud's model." she repeated.

"Really?" I asked, still having no idea what it was.

"Yes, you're all yellow from the half of your head till the face, part of your left hair is green and the rest is black. You're basically a living diagram."

"Oh!", I didn't know what else to say.

"Sorry, that was a bad analogy"

"No, it's fine. I'm sure it would have made sense to another psychology student. Are you from around here?"

"No, not at all. This is my relatives' place, I come here only during Holi. I like the celebration."

"Yeah, me too!"

We kept talking till the afternoon. My friends had gone, or to be more specific, scattered elsewhere.

The topic of conversation changed every minute, till we found a mutual topic to talk about- web series. Apparently we both loved them. She got up, and said "listen, it's lunch time, my family must be waiting, but I'll meet you soon". I smiled and nodded. I didn't have my phone with me to ask my friends where they were. It's never a good idea to bring your phone with you on Holi, so I left it at home. But I waited for an hour, then another, till the sun went down, but I never saw her that day. I wanted to talk more about the list of web series she watched. I wanted to continue that conversation.

"Samiksha, she had said. But I didn't ask her last name", I replied

"Ask Kavya, she was there on day of Holi, right?"

"Already did, she doesn't know any Samiksha either."

To be honest, I wasn't obsessed with finding her. But I don't like it when things are left haphazard. She was on my mind for a couple of days but it was temporary, I didn't even see her face, it was covered with colors.

"Just let it be," Kavya said one day, "you'll meet her someday, maybe, accidentally again. Or maybe she'll pop-up on your suggested account list." Yes, I had given up actually. But I just wanted to have that last conversation.

Eventually March 2019 arrived and so did Holi again. On this specific day, my friends called me on my phone in the morning, but I was busy collecting all the colors. My friends tried on my other number, I looked at the colors I had with me, yellow, red and dark blue. My roommate had already left, thinking I would join him later, but it had been an hour since I kept thinking of what she said, I was yellow from the head till the half part, a part of my hair was red and the rest was black. My roommate retraced his path back to the room looking for me but I wasn't there.

I was waiting outside the same apartment, coloring myself in the same way on the day we met in the hope she would recognise me in an instant. Dozens of people passed by, but I knew it was a dumb idea, but I had to try. It was just minutes before my friends found me and lectured me about all this. I sighed and went to get a sharbat, the sun was killing me. I got the feeling that someone was following me into the crowd. I turned around, I recognised that smile.

"Hey! You look familiar. Have we met before?", she asked.

I know we leave a few things for destiny to decide, the things we can't get a hold of.

But if we leave too many things to our destiny, everything starts getting mixed up.

The best we can do is take a step forward and have faith in the universe with what colors it paints us with, everyday.

20. In Search Of Some Magic Beans

I'm lost on an island with a bottle in the sea. The letter read, 'The bottle has magic beans. Plant them if you're stuck.' I'm not sure how someone can pull a prank in the sea.

Skeptical, I kept it aside and waited for help. The ships didn't seem to notice me, the fire didn't help either. Besides, I needed warmth at night, so I put it out. It was one of those days when you feel lost and thus, you are.

I cracked open the bottle under the deadly sun and planted them. I went to sleep hungry. I opened my eyes to a tree bigger than me. It had been blocking the sunlight for four hours.

'How did you end up here?' I might have been hallucinating when I heard the tree speak. But it was speaking to me. 'My ship wrecked down miles before it could reach the island'.

We kept talking on the island for the entire day when the tree said, 'What if you were stuck in the middle of the sea?'

'Well, that would be different, I would have my flares with me.'

'Is there a chance any one of those could have survived the water?'

Now that I started to think about it, there was a chance the flares could still work if I left it under sunlight to dry. 'But it's no use, the ship died far and maybe deep.'

'Buddy, you can't know it won't work if you don't dive head first.'

Maybe the tree was right. Maybe I was still hallucinating and talking to myself. But if there was any chance to get off the island, I had to take it. And so, I went down diving to search for my old ship. Maybe it was my fault, I thought. But I didn't bat an eye to repair it any sooner.

A lot of soul drenched hours later, I found one flare floating near the other end of the island but I still couldn't find my ship. And so, I returned to the tree to see if it could still talk.

And it did talk. In fact it asked me to wait till the night. The flares were majorly noticeable in the dark and you use them when you see a big ship to send a signal for help. But it was a lot of waiting for a ship to pass by and I was getting tired of the nights I slept after having to eat only beans.

One such night, when I was sleeping with my soul drooling over the sand, the island was illuminated both by the moon and a passenger ship close by the island. The tree woke me up moments before the ship could cross the island. I opened my eyes and clenched the bottle in my hand tighter. That was the only weapon I had in the lonely land. With all my faith, I lighted the only flare I had. The chilly night kept taking away the fire off the island. But it finally sparked. I held it with my limbs as high as possible. A metal sound followed the change in the ship's direction.

'I think they saw you', the tree spoke out, breaking the long silence, 'you must go.'

It was nearly dawn at that point.

'You know, if it was just a few hours later', I collected my belongings, 'the ship might have just missed us.'

There was just an extra thing I carried out of that Island, the bottle with the letter and some beans in it.

'I wish you merry on your voyage', was the last thing I heard before I left.

Before the passenger ship reached its destination, I threw the bottle in the sea again. Again, I'm not sure if I was talking to a tree, but the bottle belonged to the sea.

A week later the bottle reached a deserted island. The lost man found the bottle and opened the cork. The letter read 'The bottle has magic beans. Plant them if you're stuck.'

Share your magic beans. Share your words if they help others. Sometimes your own words which don't seem to reach you, can reach others. And if they do, I'm sure you'll start to listen to your words again.

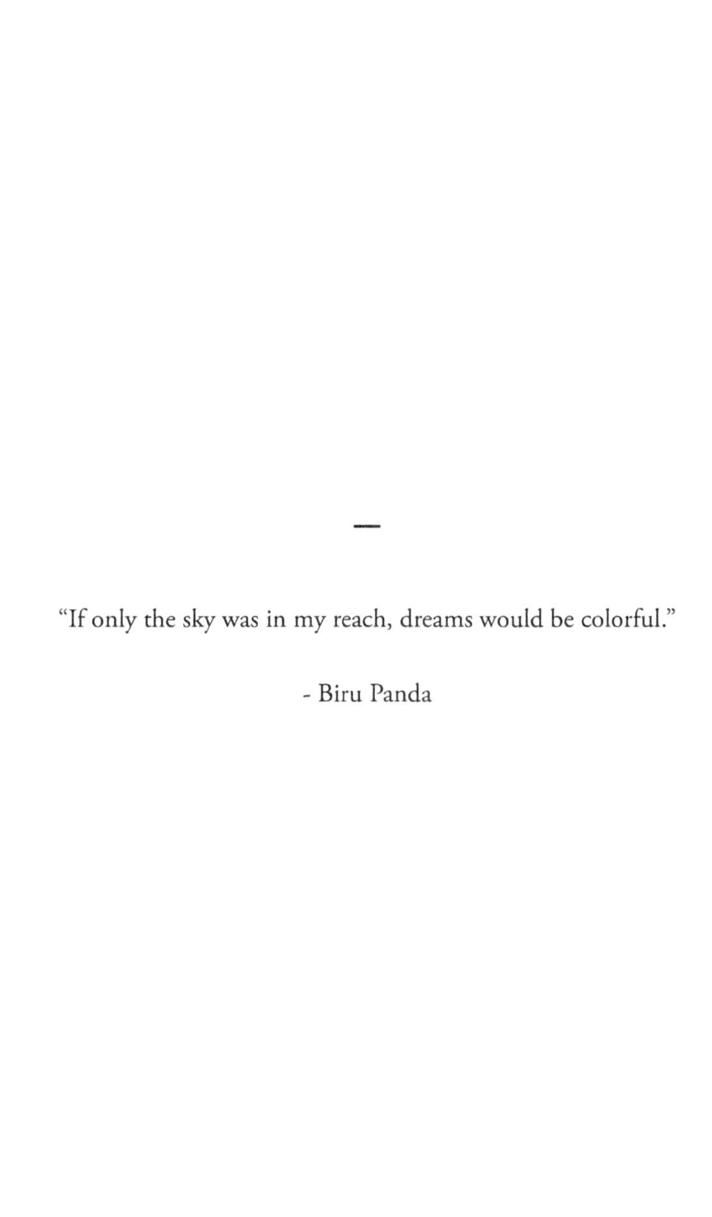

—

"If only the sky was in my reach, dreams would be colorful."

\- Biru Panda

21. Waiting For Your Letter

April 2002 : I've been exchanging letters with you for years now, my pen-friend. The old letters still lie here on my desk, untethered by dust and the occasional wind that touches it. I don't know why I haven't kept them inside my cupboard, maybe I want to keep reading them this night.

Years ago, I used to shuffle up the letters before I could even find the previous one. The rainy days were hard to pass by. I would receive the letters quite late and some of them were unreadable; the corners stained in rain and dust. We had to stop writing each other until the season passed. And that was the reason, every year I forgot about you when it rained, which is ironic because as I've mentioned in my previous letters, I love the rain. I love how it falls, touches the ground and radiates that sweet smell of 'petrichor'. And I remember you asking me, what does it mean in the next letter as well. And I apologise to reply you when the petrichor was long gone for both of us.

The last letter you wrote also mentioned that you had a vague idea of how I looked. And before I could even whisper 'how' to myself, the letter went to answer this as well, "I know you by the ways you describe things, the passion for which you write me back and expect good things. You look out for the letters I wrote, even though they're drenched, and the ink has bled into the paper far too deep to read it. You still write back after the rain about how your weeks went by in these months. I think I know how you look before we meet, because I know how to describe your soul."

This envelope I received had a sketch. A single sheet of paper. A hand drawn half shaded portrait face, with the words written just below it, "this is the only letter I'm not afraid to write in the rain."

22. Chaotically Cloudy

There are times
I am lost in your eyes
Thinking it to be the sun
For you shine too bright sometimes
I must look away
for a brief moment
The rain on the other side
Envys me on occasions
For it wants to drip where
you shine the brightest
Mountains and lillies sing to you
When you keep the rain at bay
And I stare into your eyes
For bringing the sun.

23. Tragedies of the Heart

We don't have the entirety of our hearts with us.
We look for it in people and places
and those who can't find it, give up.
But that's the real tragedy, isn't it?
To think that the kind of happiness we look for
can only be found by searching for it
and not sharing it with people we love.

Hearts live in tragedy.
Too little of something and it suffers.
Too much of something and it suffers.
Hearts will have only one moment of relief
and then it'll suffer.
It's inevitable.
But why do you ask if that will stop me
from wanting you forever?

The real reason
heart is claimed as a tragedy
is because it only feels.
It does not choose.

I wonder why hearts live in cages.
I wonder what they make us want to do
when they feel the warmth of
another miserable heart
inching away from us.

How close do you want our hearts to be?
Even if we melt into each other
to bridge the gap between us,
our hearts will always beat at different rhythms.

—

"Sometimes I don't remember how I met my close ones. For a moment I completely space out about the past. But between the time I'm not able to remember how we met and the time when I figure it out, they don't feel like strangers to me, not even for a moment."

- Biru Panda

About The Writer

Biru Panda is from Bhubaneswar, Odisha. He writes about longings and loves to connect the dots. He loves writing about out-of-the-box plot lines including short stories and poems. He turns everyone he meets into words in his work. You can connect with him on instagram (@onelastscribble) / E-mail (birupanda9@gmail.com).

Something To Scribble On